Letts

KS1

VISUAL REVISION GUIDE

SUCCESS

QUESTIONS & ANSWERS

MATHEMATICS

Author
Paul Broadbent

CONTENTS

NUMBERS

CALCULATIONS

GRAPHS AND CHARTS

MEASURES AND SHAPES

TEST, ANSWERS, USEFUL WORDS

3

PERFECT PATTERNS

COUNTING OBJECTS

Draw circles around these bugs to group them into 2s. Write down how many groups there are, and how many bugs.

9 groups of 2 = 18 bugs

COUNTING TO 100

This number square has some numbers missing.

Write in all the missing numbers.

0	1	2	3	4	5	6	7	8	9
10	11	12	13	14	15	16	17	18	19
20	21	22	23	24	25	26	27	28	29
30	31	32	33	34	35	36	37	38	39
40	41	42	43	44	45	46	47	48	49
50	51	52	53	54	55	56	57	58	59
60	61	62	63	64	65	66	67	68	69
70	71	72	73	74	75	76	77	78	79
80	81	82	83	84	85	86	87	88	89
90	91	92	93	94	95	96	97	98	99

SEQUENCES

Write down the missing numbers in these sequences.

1 17 18 | 19 | | 20 | 21 22 23 | 24 |

2 46 | 47 | 48 49 | 50 | | 51 | 52 | 53 |

3 32 31 | 30 | 29 | 28 | | 27 | 26 | 25 |

4 | 86 | | 85 | 84 83 | 82 | 81 | 80 | | 79 |

Oh no, I hate bugs!

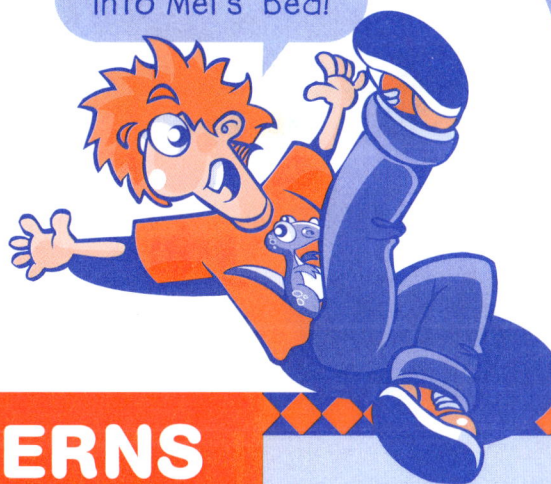

I might make some of these bugs go missing – into Mel's bed!

NUMBER PATTERNS

1 Counting in 2s, show the jumps and circle the numbers.

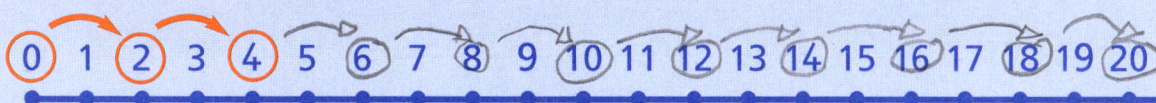

⓪ 1 ② 3 ④ 5 ⑥ 7 ⑧ 9 ⑩ 11 ⑫ 13 ⑭ 15 ⑯ 17 ⑱ 19 ⑳

2 Counting in 5s, write the next four numbers.

(15) — (20) — (25) — (30) — (35) — (40) — (45)

3 Counting in 3s, write the next four numbers.

(3) — (6) — (9) — (12) — (15) — (18) — (21)

TEEN NUMBERS

Write these numbers as words to find a hidden number.

16 → | S | i | x | t | e | e | n |

12 → | | t | w | e | l | v | e |

14 → | f | o | u | r | t | e | e | n |

17 → | | | S | e | v | e | n | t | e | e | n |

13 → | t | h | i | r | t | e | e | n |

19 → | | n | i | n | e | t | e | e | n |

The hidden number is | 11 | .

NIFTY NUMBERS

2-DIGIT NUMBERS

Write down the numbers shown by each abacus.

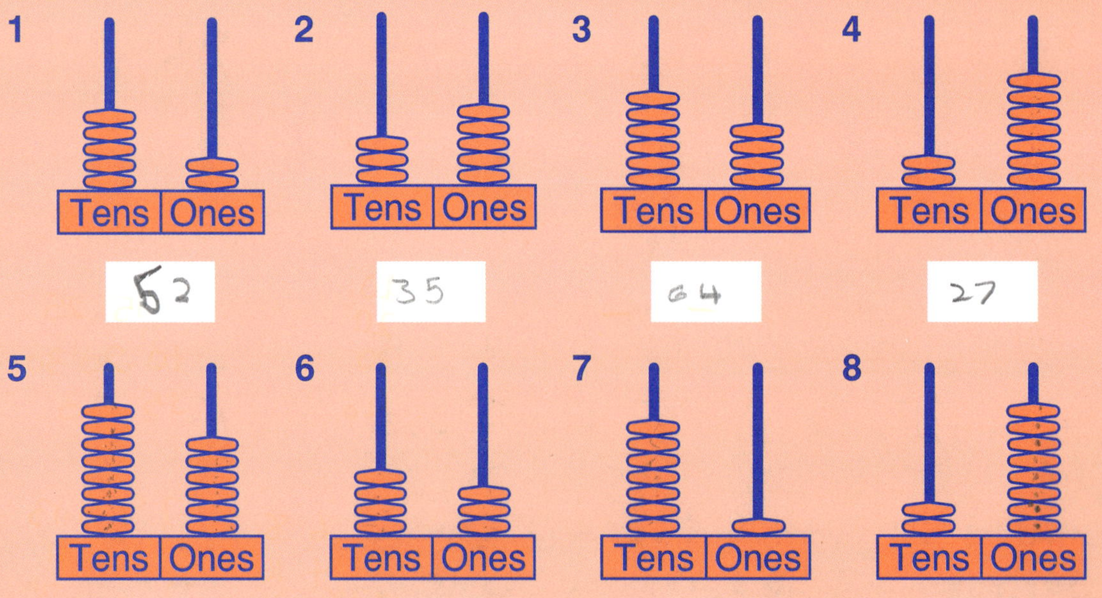

1 Tens Ones   52

2 Tens Ones   35

3 Tens Ones   64

4 Tens Ones   27

5 Tens Ones   86

6 Tens Ones   483

7 Tens Ones   71

8 Tens Ones   28

3-DIGIT NUMBERS

Fill in the boxes to complete these sums.

1 487 = 400 + 80 + 7

2 394 = 300 + 90 + 4

3 269 = 200 + 60 + 9

4 735 = 700 + 30 + 5

5 918 = 900 + 10 + 8

6 842 = 800 + 40 + 2

ODD AND EVEN NUMBERS

Circle all the even numbers.

50   54   31

26   25

47   32

18

Sam is odd!

I'll get even with Mel for that!

MULTIPLES

Write the numbers from 1 to 40 in the correct place on this Carroll diagram. The first few numbers have been written in for you.

What do you notice about the numbers here?

	multiple of 2	not a multiple of 2
multiple of 5	10 20 30 40	5 15 25 10 20 30 35 40
not a multiple of 5	2 6 8 12 14 16 18 38 4 36 22 24 26 28 32 34	7 9 11 13 33 29 31 37 1 17 19 3 39 21 23 27

7

COMPARING AND ORDERING

FIRST THINGS FIRST

Draw a line to join each position to the correct car.

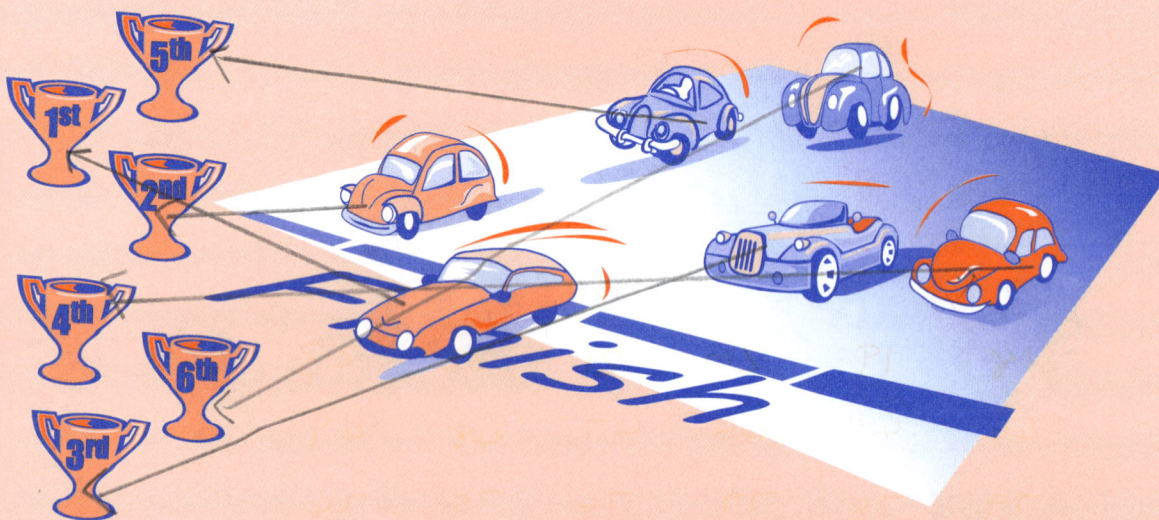

COMPARING NUMBERS

Circle the bigger number in each pair.

1 34 (43)   2 (81) 79   3 92 (95)   4 68 (86)
5 57 (64)   6 19 (91)   7 (72) 69   8 (87) 84

HALFWAY NUMBERS

Fill in the number in the middle of each pair.

1 17– 21 –25   2 32– 35 –38
3 51– 54 –57   4 14– 20 –26

8

ORDERING NUMBERS

Write these sets of numbers in order, starting with the smallest.

1 27 24 30 31 25 19

19	24	25	27	30	31

2 58 85 47 52 83 60

47	52	58	60	83	85

COMPARING NUMBERS

Fill in the numbers that come between each pair.

1 17	18	19	20	21	22	23	24
2 43	44	45	46	47	48	49	50
3 80	79	78	77	76	75	74	73
4 66	65	64	63	62	61	60	59

We've been playing golf and I had more shots than Mel.

That means I came first with the lowest score!

top tip
Number tracks and hundred squares are very useful for helping to learn the order of numbers.

9

ESTIMATING AND ROUNDING

GOOD ESTIMATES

- Look at each of these sets.

- Without counting them, estimate how many there are in each set. Write your estimates in the boxes.

- Once you have done this, count the sets. How close was your estimate?

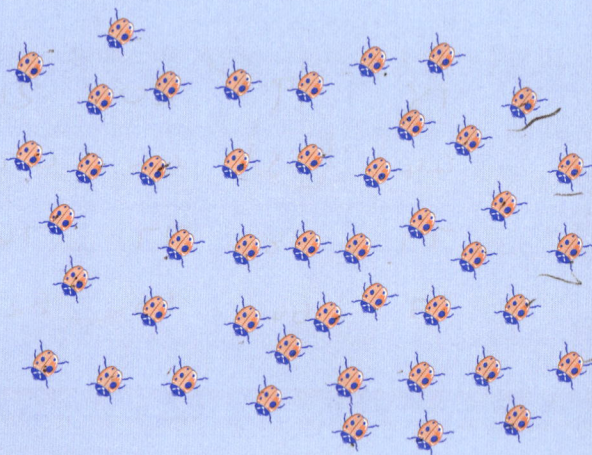

Estimate → 21

Count → 84

Estimate → 50

Count → 46.

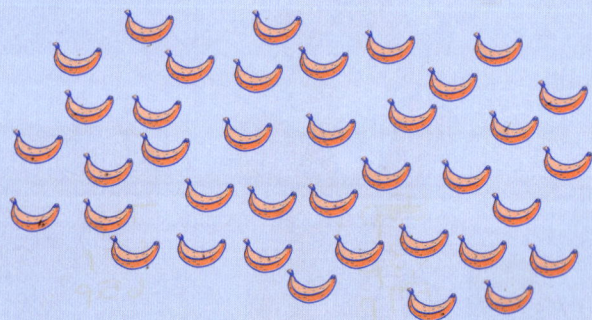

Estimate → 16

Count → 17

Estimate → 20.

Count → 38.

NUMBER LINES

Estimate the number shown by each arrow. Write your estimates in the boxes.

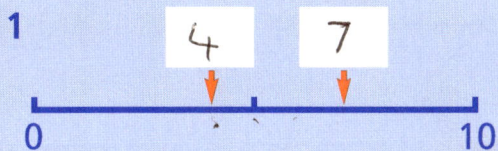

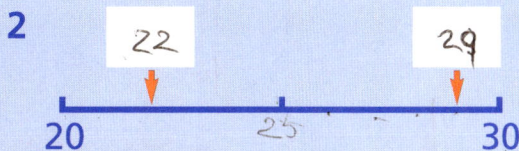

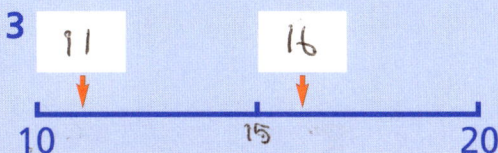

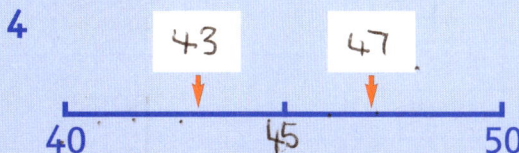

1 ┌───┐ ┌───┐
     │ 4 │ │ 7 │
     └───┘ └───┘
0 ──────────────── 10

2 ┌────┐ ┌────┐
     │ 22 │ │ 29 │
     └────┘ └────┘
20 ──────25──────── 30

3 ┌────┐ ┌────┐
     │ 11 │ │ 16 │
     └────┘ └────┘
10 ────15──────── 20

4 ┌────┐ ┌────┐
     │ 43 │ │ 47 │
     └────┘ └────┘
40 ──────45──────── 50

ROUNDING

Round these amounts to the nearest 10p.

Write the amounts in the correct bags.

top tip
If a number ends in 5 or more, it rounds up to the next 10. If it is less than 5, it rounds down and the 10 stays the same.

63p   57p   71p   Round to 80

66p   84p   81p
    76p

65p   55p

50 51 52 53 54 (55) 56 57 58 59 (60) 61 62 63
64 (65)

(bag: 81p, 84p, 76p)

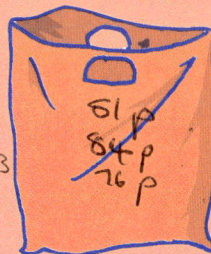

I think I'll round that down to 20p!

Round to 60   **Round to 70**

(bag: 65p, 63p, 57p)   *(bag: 71p, 66p, 65p)*

Sam owes me 22p.

FRACTIONS OF SHAPES

1 Colour ½ of each shape.

2 Colour ¼ of each shape.

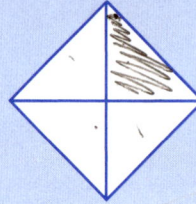

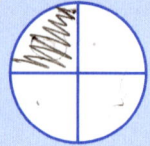

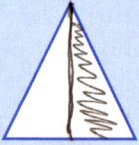

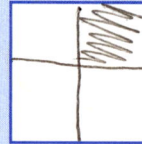

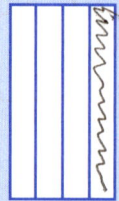

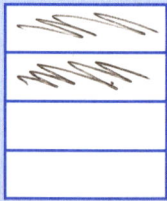

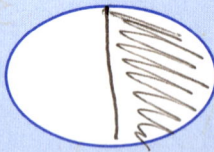

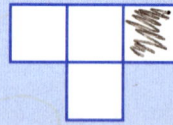

FRACTION FRENZY

EQUAL PARTS

Tick the shapes that show quarters.

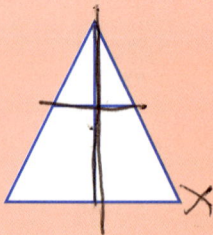

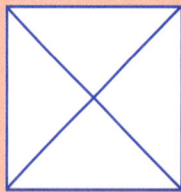

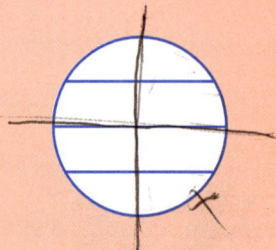

top tip
Remember, if a shape is cut into quarters it is cut into 4 equal parts.

12

FRACTIONS OF AMOUNTS

Write down $\frac{1}{2}$ of each of these numbers.

Colour the sweets to help you.

1 $\frac{1}{2}$ of 6 = 3

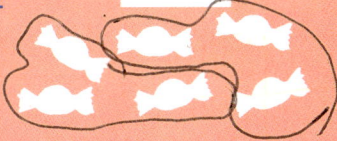

2 $\frac{1}{2}$ of 10 = 5

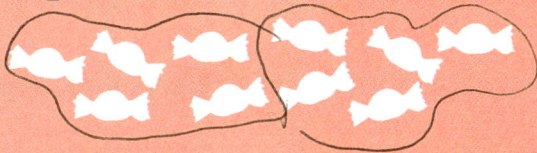

3 $\frac{1}{2}$ of 8 = 4

4 $\frac{1}{2}$ of 12 = 6

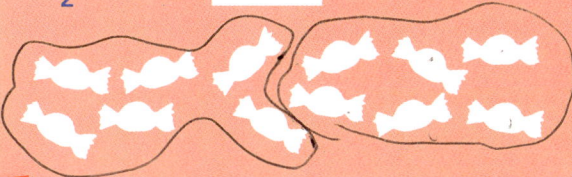

Write down $\frac{1}{4}$ of each of these numbers.

Colour the sweets to help you.

5 $\frac{1}{4}$ of 8 = 2

6 $\frac{1}{4}$ of 12 = 3

7 $\frac{1}{4}$ of 20 = 5

8 $\frac{1}{4}$ of 16 = 4

4+4=8 - 8+8=16.

Mel, I have 12 sweets. Would you like a $\frac{1}{4}$ of them?

Give me $\frac{1}{2}$ a minute to work this out.

NUMBER INVESTIGATION

COMPLETE THE SQUARE

This 100-square is a little different to normal.

- Write in these numbers first:

  39 60 9 18 99 25 75 56.

- Now write in all the other numbers to complete the square.

		97		95	94	93			
		88	87			84		82	81
80	79	78		76					
70			67	66			63		61
		58				54	53		51
	49	48			45			42	41
			37	36	35				
30		28				24		22	
	19		17				13		11
10			7	6		4	3	2	1

Why was Dracula good with numbers?

Because he was a Count!

14

AND THIS ONE!

Here's another 100-square that's a bit different.

- Write in these numbers first:

  73 37 98 23 8 51 14 65.

- Now complete the square by writing in all the other numbers.

1	20		40			61			100
2	19	22		42		62	79	82	
3			38		58	63		83	
		24		44			77	84	
	16		36					85	
6	15	26					75		95
7		27		47	54				
			33					88	93
	12		32			69			
10	11	30		50	51	70	71		91

STUDYING THE SQUARES

top tip

Remember, even numbers always end in the digits 0, 2, 4, 6, or 8.

For both 100-squares:

- colour the even numbers red
- look at the patterns on each of them.

FASCINATING FACTS

TOTALS TO 10

Look at the number in the centre of each circle. Now fill in the boxes to make this number in different ways.

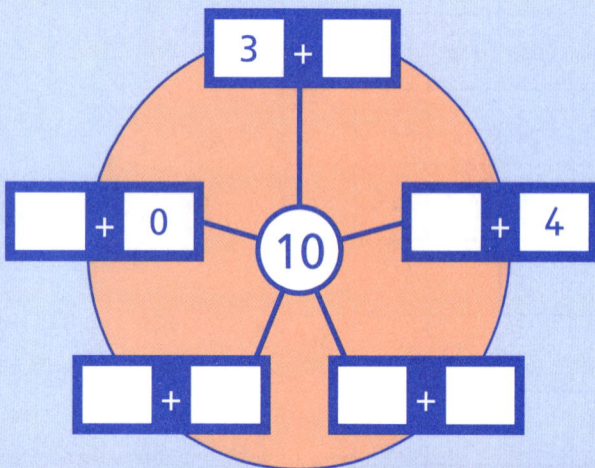

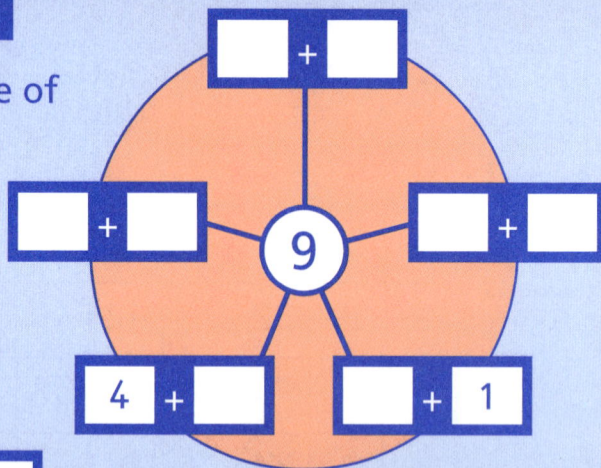

[ ] + [ ]

[ ] + [ ]   (9)   [ ] + [ ]

4 + [ ]   [ ] + 1

3 + [ ]

[ ] + 0   (10)   [ ] + 4

[ ] + [ ]   [ ] + [ ]

top tip
Remember that 4 + 3 gives the same answer as 3 + 4. It doesn't matter which way round you add.

TRIOS

These trios make different number facts.

Fill in each of the facts with the numbers given.

1 4   7
      11

4 + [ ] = 11   11 − [ ] = 4

7 + [ ] = [ ]   [ ] − 4 = [ ]

2 8   6
      14

[ ] + [ ] = [ ]   [ ] − [ ] = [ ]

[ ] + [ ] = [ ]   [ ] + [ ] = [ ]

3 9   7
      16

[ ] + [ ] = [ ]   [ ] − [ ] = [ ]

[ ] + [ ] = [ ]   [ ] − [ ] = [ ]

16

NUMBER BONDS

Write down the answers to each of these questions. Then use the code to find five vegetables.

CODE	N	P	O	A	S	I	C	U	R	T
	8	9	10	11	12	13	14	15	16	17

1 9 + 5 = 14   C

18 – 7 = ☐ ____

8 + 8 = ☐ ____

11 + 5 = ☐ ____

19 – 9 = ☐ ____

8 + 9 = ☐ ____

2 11 + 6 = ☐ ____

7 + 8 = ☐ ____

9 + 7 = ☐ ____

14 – 6 = ☐ ____

18 – 5 = ☐ ____

17 – 8 = ☐ ____

3 14 – 5 = ☐ ____

6 + 4 = ☐ ____

12 + 5 = ☐ ____

17 – 6 = ☐ ____

13 + 4 = ☐ ____

18 – 8 = ☐ ____

4 18 – 6 = ☐ ____

20 – 11 = ☐ ____

7 + 9 = ☐ ____

3 + 7 = ☐ ____

9 + 6 = ☐ ____

6 + 11 = ☐ ____

17 – 5 = ☐ ____

5 13 – 4 = ☐ ____

20 – 9 = ☐ ____

9 + 7 = ☐ ____

4 + 8 = ☐ ____

17 – 9 = ☐ ____

6 + 7 = ☐ ____

16 – 7 = ☐ ____

What will I make if I put a slice of bread on each side of my face?

A Sam-wich!

17

BIG NUMBERS

Complete these number trails by writing in the answer to each sum.

		+40		+80		−20		+50		−60	
1	10	→		→		→		→		→	100

		+70		−50		+90		−80		+60	
2	10	→		→		→		→		→	100

		+400		−200		+900		+700		−900	
3	100	→		→		→		→		→	1000

		+600		+100		−500		−100		+800	
4	100	→		→		→		→		→	1000

ADDING AND TAKING AWAY

What would happen if I went into the doubling machine?

USING DOUBLES

Write the numbers coming out of the doubling machine.

Use these to help answer the questions.

1 14		14 + 15 =	
2 21		21 + 22 =	
3 60		60 + 59 =	
4 35		35 + 36 =	
5 25		25 + 24 =	
6 40		40 + 41 =	

IN DOUBLE OUT

Double trouble!

ROUNDING

Draw a line to join each calculation to the correct answer.

14 + 19   17 – 9   46 – 19   23 + 9

26 – 9

15 + 9

24   **27**   **8**   **17**   **32**   **33**

36 – 19

27 – 19   42 – 9   33 – 9   18 + 9

13 + 19

top tip

If you need to add or take away 9, round it to 10 to make it easier, e.g. 14–9 is 14–10 and then add 1, which is 5.

You can do this to add or take away 19, 29, 39 ...

ADDING 2-DIGIT NUMBERS

Fill in the answer to each question. Colour the star for any you found easy.

1 18 + 25 = ☆   **2** 26 + 46 = ☆   **3** 48 + 34 = ☆

4 57 + 17 = ☆   **5** 38 + 23 = ☆   **6** 51 + 37 = ☆

COUNTING ON

Use the number line to help you find the difference between these pairs of numbers. Then write the answers in the boxes.

20 ———— 30 ———— 40 ———— 50

1 27 36 →   **2** 42 28 →   **3** 32 49 →

4 21 35 →   **5** 29 48 →   **6** 24 43 →

19

MULTIPLYING AND DIVIDING

COUNTING GROUPS

Draw 3 fish in each pool. Write down how many *groups* of fish there are. Then work out the total number of fish.

1

4 × 3 =

Draw 4 flags on each castle. Write down how many groups of flags there are. Then work out the total number.

2

5 × 4 =

I'm the king of the castle!

I think you're the little rascal!

DIVIDING

Group these things, then fill in the missing numbers.

1 Group in 2s

[ ] groups of 2

$12 \div 2 = $ [ ]

4 Group in 3s

[ ] groups of 3

$12 \div 3 = $ [ ]

2 Group in 3s

[ ] groups of 3

$15 \div 3 = $ [ ]

5 Group in 5s

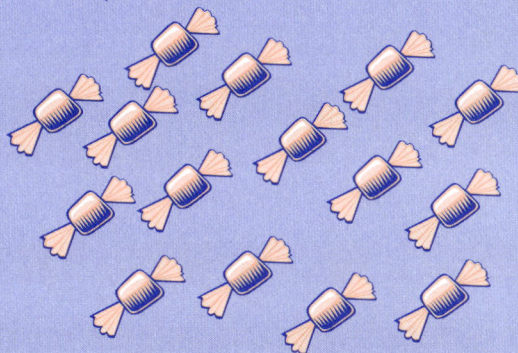

[ ] groups of 5

$15 \div 5 = $ [ ]

3 Group in 4s

[ ] groups of 4

$16 \div 4 = $ [ ]

6 Group in 4s

[ ] groups of 4

$12 \div 4 = $ [ ]

★ ★ ★ ★
★ **top tip** ★
The division sign is ÷
Dividing is the opposite to multiplying, so check your answer with multiplication.
$14 \div 2 = 7$
$7 \times 2 = 14$

TERRIFIC TIMES TABLES

CALCULATIONS

2 TIMES TABLE

1 Draw jumps of 2 on this number line. Colour the numbers that you land on.

0 1 2 3 4 5 6 7 8 9 10 11 12 13 14 15 16 17 18 19 20

2 Write in the missing numbers for these sums.

$4 \times 2 = \boxed{}$ $\boxed{} \times 2 = 14$ $2 \times \boxed{} = 6$

$5 \times \boxed{} = 10$ $2 \times \boxed{} = 18$ $8 \times 2 = \boxed{}$

$\boxed{} \times 2 = 20$ $\boxed{} \times 2 = 4$ $2 \times \boxed{} = 12$

MULTIPLYING BY 5 AND 10

Fill in the missing numbers in each table.

1 ×5

IN	3		8		7		2	
OUT	15	45		25		30		20

2 ×10

IN	6		4		9		8	
OUT	60	70		50		20		30

22

MULTIPLYING BY 3 AND 4

1 Continue to fill in these sequences.

3 → 6 → 9 → 12 → ☐ → ☐ → ☐ → ☐ → ☐ → ☐

4 → 8 → 12 → 16 → ☐ → ☐ → ☐ → ☐ → ☐ → ☐

2 Fill in the missing numbers.

$3 \times \boxed{} = 12$ $4 \times \boxed{} = 32$ $\boxed{} \times 3 = 6$

$5 \times 4 = \boxed{}$ $\boxed{} \times 7 = 21$ $4 \times \boxed{} = 36$

$9 \times \boxed{} = 27$ $6 \times \boxed{} = 24$ $8 \times 3 = \boxed{}$

TRICKY TABLES

Complete these grids by filling in the missing numbers.

1

×	3	2	5
7			
4		8	
9			

2

×	4	10	3
6			
8			
5			

3

×	8	9	7
5			
3			
4			

I'm 10 times better at everything than you, Sam!

Yes – 10 times as messy, 10 times as noisy … !

top tip

Remember that 2×6 gives the same answer as 6×2. It doesn't matter which way round it is written.

PROBLEM-SOLVING SKILLS

WORD PROBLEMS

1 9 bricks, each 10cm in length, are laid end to end in a row. What is the total length of the row?

cm

2 Laura has 28 stickers and Sam has 19 stickers. How many more stickers has Laura than Sam?

3 A football team has 14 players. If 4 players can travel in one car, how many cars are needed to take them to their matches?

4 4 egg boxes, each with 6 eggs, are dropped. 15 eggs are broken. How many eggs are left?

5 There are 25 sweets in a bag. Josh eats 6 sweets and Ryan eats twice as many as Josh. How many sweets are left?

6 Fred is $\frac{1}{5}$ of the weight of his Dad, who weighs 70kg. What does Fred weigh?

kg

MONEY TOTALS

Total these coins. First write them as pounds, then write them as pence.

1  £ [   ]   [   ] p

2  £ [   ]   [   ] p

3  £ [   ]   [   ] p

4  £ [   ]   [   ] p

GIVING CHANGE

Write the change from £1 for each of these amounts.

1 65p → change [   ] p

2 40p → change [   ] p

3 85p → change [   ] p

4 15p → change [   ] p

5 79p → change [   ] p

6 54p → change [   ] p

I'm richer than you. I've got 3 coins and you've only got 1!

No, I'm richer because your three 20p coins only makes 60p. My £1 coin is worth 100p.

MONEY INVESTIGATION

WHAT'S THE POSTAGE?

Using only 2p and 3p stamps, draw the correct postage on these postcards. Try to get up to 20p.

An example has been done for you.

2p **3p**

5p	6p	7p	8p
2p 3p			

9p	10p	11p	12p

13p	14p	15p	16p

17p	18p	19p	20p

HOW MANY COINS?

Look at each full purse. Now draw the same amount of money in the empty purse, but only use half the number of coins.

1

20p 20p 10p 2p

[4] coins → [52] p   [2] coins → [52] p

2

20p 5p 5p 20p 10p 10p

[ ] coins → [ ] p   [ ] coins → [ ] p

3

20p 20p 5p 5p 1p 2p

[ ] coins → [ ] p   [ ] coins → [ ] p

You can have half the money in my purse.

That's no good. Your purse is empty!

SORT IT OUT!

VENN DIAGRAMS

1 Sort the fruit by writing the names on this Venn diagram.

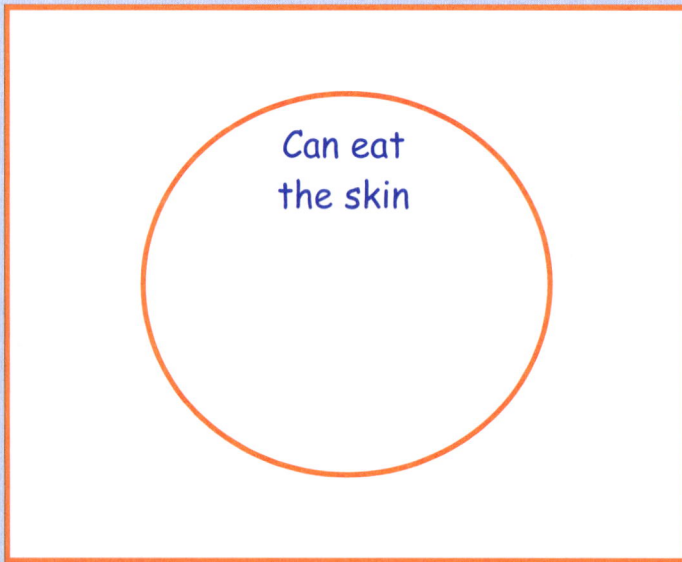

Can eat
the skin

2 Write the numbers 1 to 20 on this Venn diagram

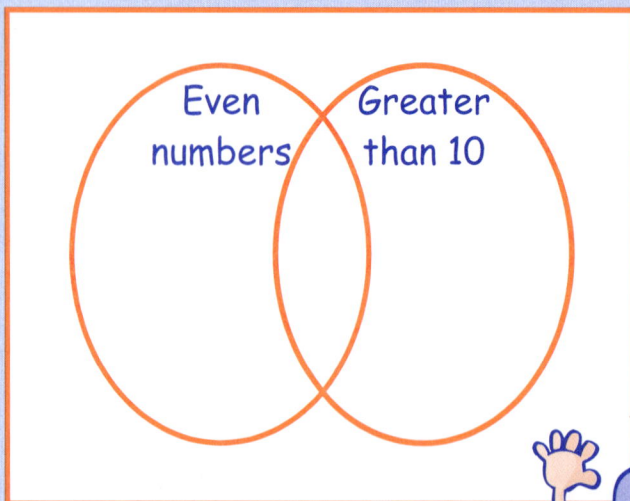

Even
numbers

Greater
than 10

How can you make a LEMON double in size?

Change its letters to make it a MELON!

CARROLL DIAGRAMS

Draw these shapes on this Carroll diagram.

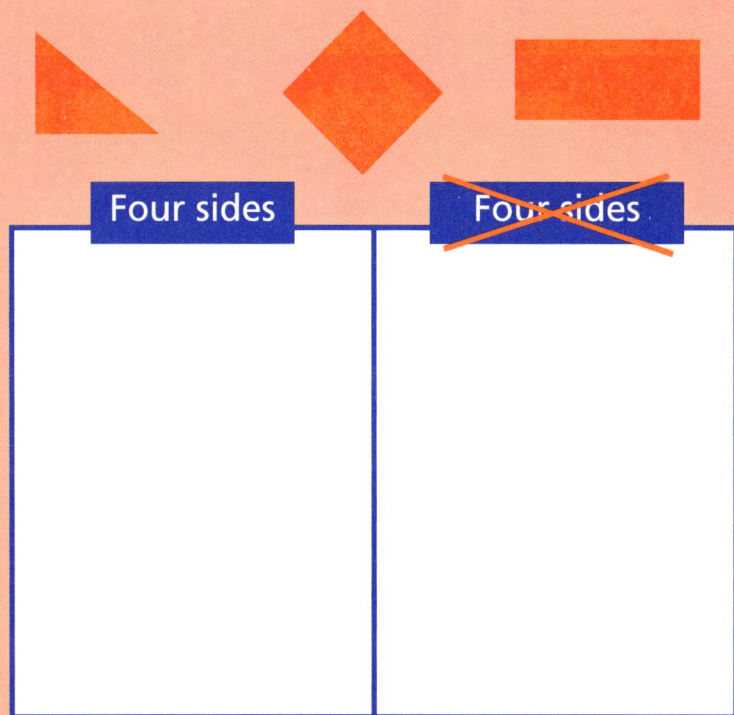

Four sides	~~Four sides~~

top tip
In Carroll diagrams one 'label' is always the opposite of another. So this has 'four sides' and 'not four sides' as the labels. The crossing out shows that shapes that do not have four sides go in this part of the diagram.

TREE DIAGRAMS

Look at this tree diagram.

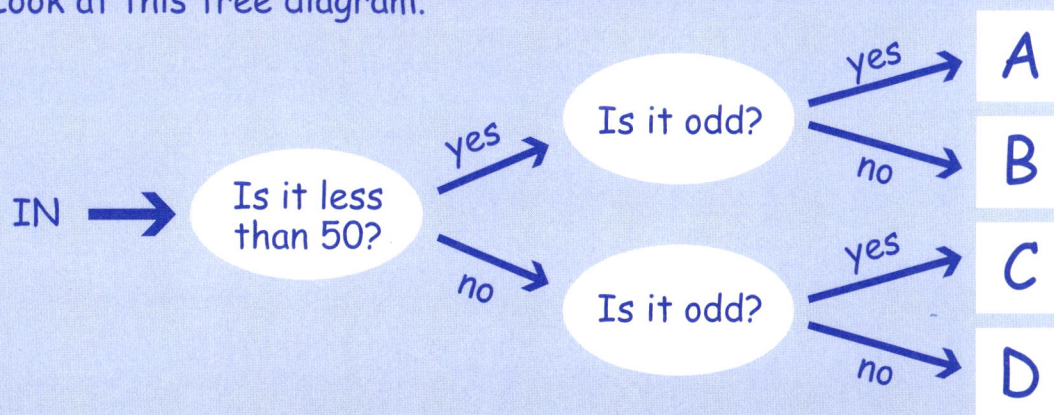

IN → Is it less than 50?
- yes → Is it odd? — yes → A / no → B
- no → Is it odd? — yes → C / no → D

Write down which boxes these numbers would be sorted into.

1 18 → ☐   2 65 → ☐   3 7 → ☐

4 94 → ☐   5 100 → ☐   6 21 → ☐

29

GREGARIOUS GRAPHS

PICTOGRAMS

This pictogram shows the number of books read by a group of children in one month.

Emma	📖 📖 📖 📖 📖
David	📖 📖 📖 📖
Sian	📖 📖 📖 📖 📖 📖 📖 📖 📖 📖 📖 📖
Josh	📖 📖 📖 📖 📖 📖 📖 📖 📖 📖
Katy	📖 📖 📖 📖
Ben	📖 📖 📖 📖 📖 📖 📖

Key
📖
is 1 book

1 How many books did Josh read?

2 Who read 7 books in this month?

3 How many more books did Sian read than Katy?

4 Which 2 children read the same number of books?

5 How many books did Emma and Ben read altogether?

6 How many children read more than 5 books in this month?

BLOCK GRAPHS

This graph shows how a class of children travel to school.

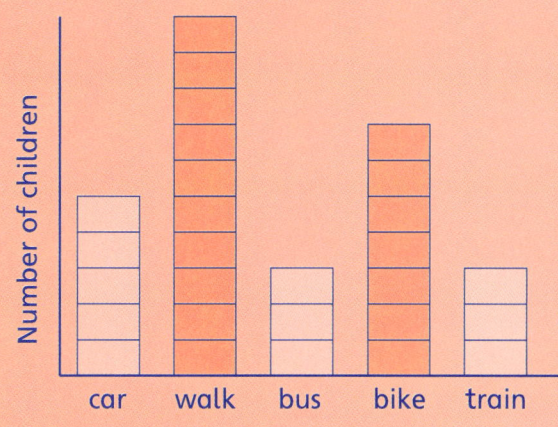

How do you travel to school, Mel?

Slowly!

Number of children

car walk bus bike train

1 How many children travelled by car?

2 How many more children walked than cycled?

3 How many children did not walk or cycle?

4 How many children are there altogether in the class?

BAR CHARTS

This graph shows the time Daniel took to travel to school each day for a week.

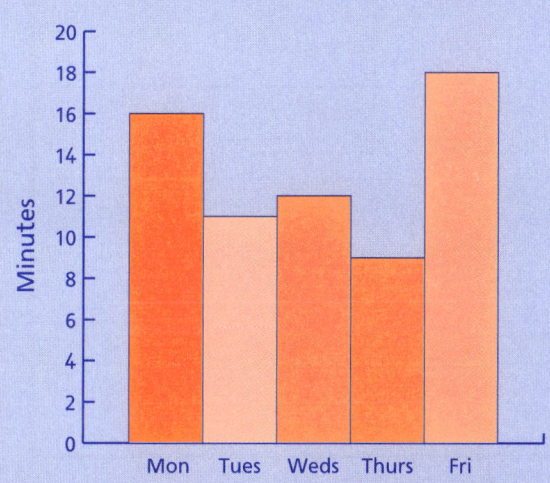

Minutes

20
18
16
14
12
10
8
6
4
2
0

Mon Tues Weds Thurs Fri

1 On which day did he take 11 minutes? _____

2 How many minutes was his journey on Thursday? _____

3 How much longer did it take him to travel on Friday than on Wednesday? _____

4 Which day took 5 minutes longer than travelling on Tuesday? _____

GRAPH INVESTIGATION

GATHERING INFORMATION

- Choose one of your reading books and open it on any page.

- Count the number of letters for each of the words on the page. For example, the word GRAPH has 5 letters.

- Keep a tally to show the number of words with 1 letter, the number of words with 2 letters, and so on. Your tally will be easier to count if you use ⊞ ⊞ .

top tip
Draw the tally in groups of 5. ⊞ shows 5. It makes it easy to count.

Number of letters	Tally of words
1	
2	
3	
4	
5	
6	
7	
8 or more	

PLOTTING YOUR GRAPH

Draw a bar graph to show the number of words for each letter count.

Use your tally chart opposite to draw the graph.

Decide on the scale of your graph.

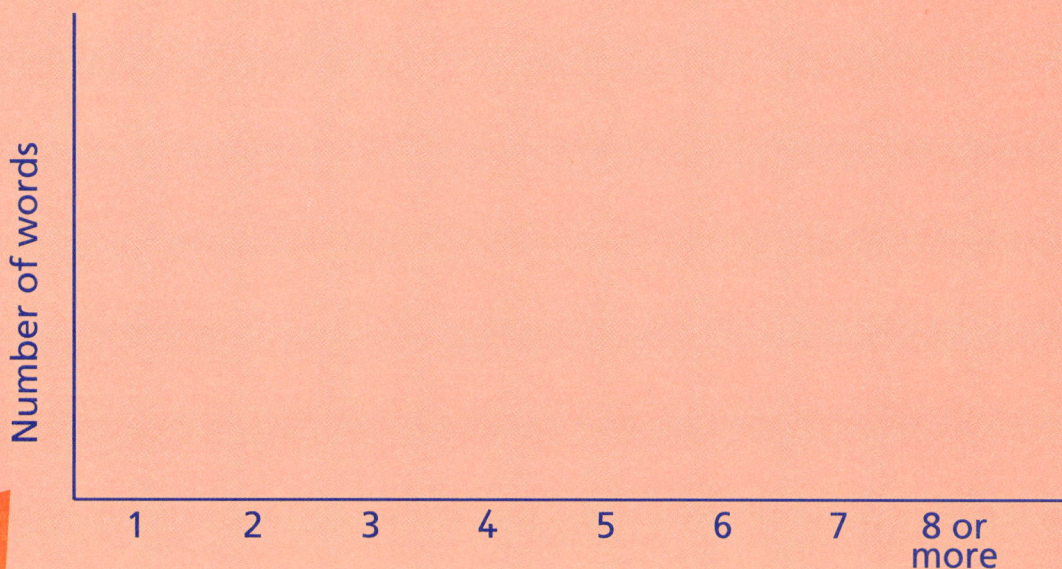

Number of words

| 1 | 2 | 3 | 4 | 5 | 6 | 7 | 8 or more |

USING YOUR GRAPH

Use your graph to answer these questions.

1 What is the most common length of word?

2 What is the least common length of word?

Can you make a sentence with only 3-letter words?

Mel and Sam ate ham and red jam for tea!

UNITS OF MEASUREMENT

Draw a line to join each item to the correct unit of measurement.

30kg

centimetres

metres

millilitres

litres

grams

kilograms

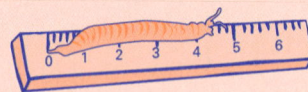

MIGHTY MEASUREMENT

I have to measure everything carefully so Mel doesn't get more than me.

I'll give you 50mm of this liquorice and I'll only have 10cm myself!

34

HEAVIER OR LIGHTER?

Circle the objects that you think weigh more than 1 kilogram.

LONGER OR SHORTER?

How long do you think that each of these pencils is? First, write down your estimate. Then measure the pencil for the exact length.

1
Estimate _____ cm
Exact length _____ cm

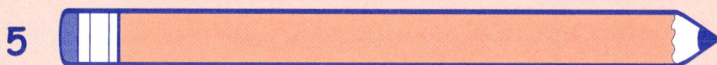

2
Estimate _____ cm
Exact length _____ cm

3
Estimate _____ cm
Exact length _____ cm

4
Estimate _____ cm
Exact length _____ cm

5
Estimate _____ cm
Exact length _____ cm

THE TEST OF TIME

TIME FACTS

1 Fill in the missing information about times.

☐ minutes = 1 hour	☐ days = 1 week
☐ months = 1 year	☐ seconds = 1 minute
☐ hours = 1 day	☐ weeks = 1 year

2 Complete this puzzle grid by writing in the other six days of the week.

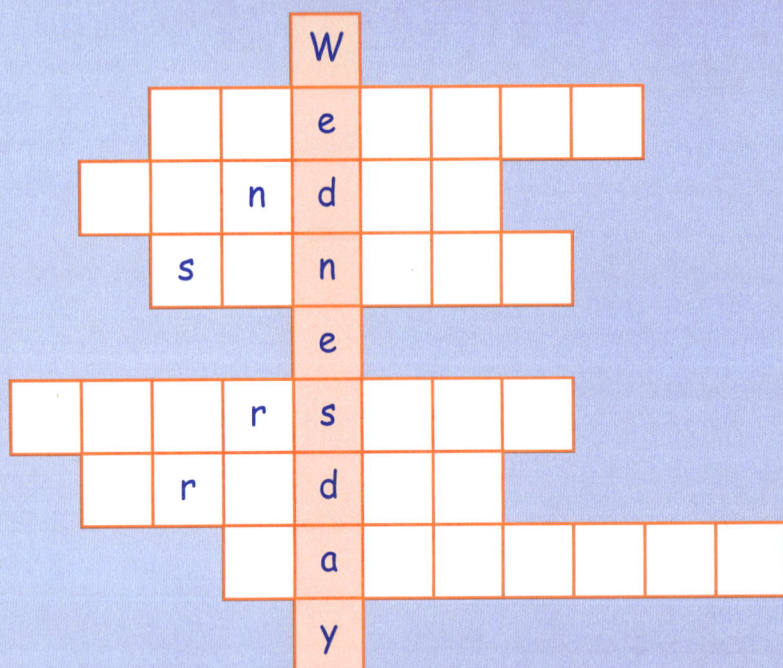

W
e
n d
s n n
e
r s
r d
a
y

3 Write out the months of the year in the correct order.

Spring	Summer	Autumn	Winter
M	J	S	D
A	J	O	J
M	A	N	F

READING THE TIME

Write down the times shown on each of these clocks.

1
2
3

4
5
6
7

Draw the hands on these clocks to show the times.

1
2

`7:15`   `11:30`

What has a face but no eyes and hands but no arms?

3
4

`4:00`   `1:45`

A clock!

37

SHAPING UP

SHAPE NAMES

Draw a line to join each shape to its name.

cuboid

pentagon

triangle

sphere

cone

hexagon

pyramid

octagon

quadrilateral

cylinder

cube

heptagon

An ice-cream!

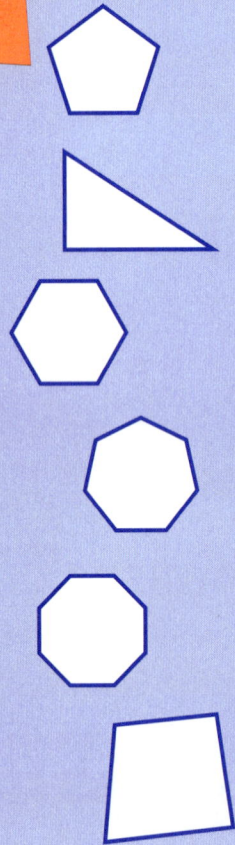

My favourite treat is a cone with a sphere on top. What is it?

SORTING SHAPES

Draw the shapes in the correct parts of each diagram.

1

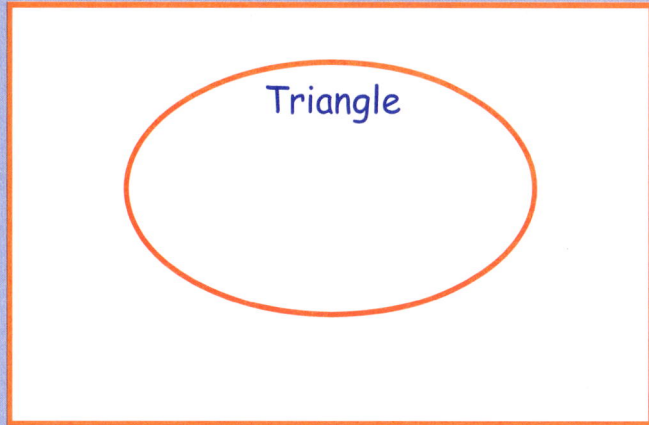

Triangle

2

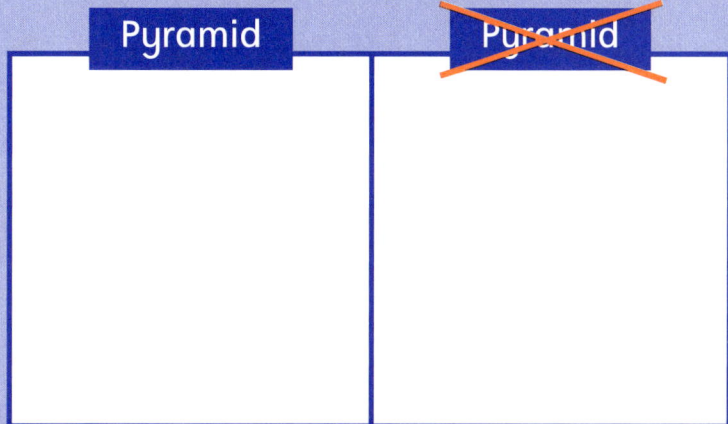

Pyramid   ~~Pyramid~~

SYMMETRY

Draw a line of symmetry on each shape.

top tip

A line of symmetry is like a fold line.

If you imagine a symmetrical shape folded down the middle, the two sides would match.

39

POSITION AND TURNING

GRIDS

1 Look at this plan. Then write down what is at each of these positions.

B6 →

E2 →

A4 →

B3 →

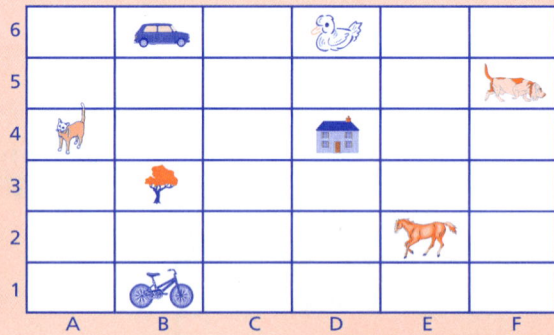

2 Now write down the positions of these.

🚲 →

🐕 →

🏠 →

🐤 →

> A right angle is a quarter turn.

> I wonder what a wrong angle is?

RIGHT ANGLES

Tick the right angles on each of these shapes.

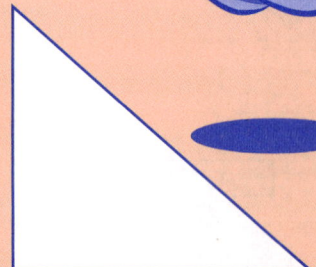

40

DIRECTIONS

top tip
Remember, clockwise moves in the direction of clock hands and anti-clockwise goes in the opposite direction.

Write down where Sam will be facing after these turns.

Start position	Turn	Finish position
1 Facing the church	$\frac{1}{4}$ turn clockwise	
2 Facing the park	$\frac{1}{4}$ turn anti-clockwise	
3 Facing the school	$\frac{1}{2}$ turn clockwise	
4 Facing home	$\frac{1}{2}$ turn anti-clockwise	

POINTS OF THE COMPASS

Fill in these words to tell you the points of a compass.

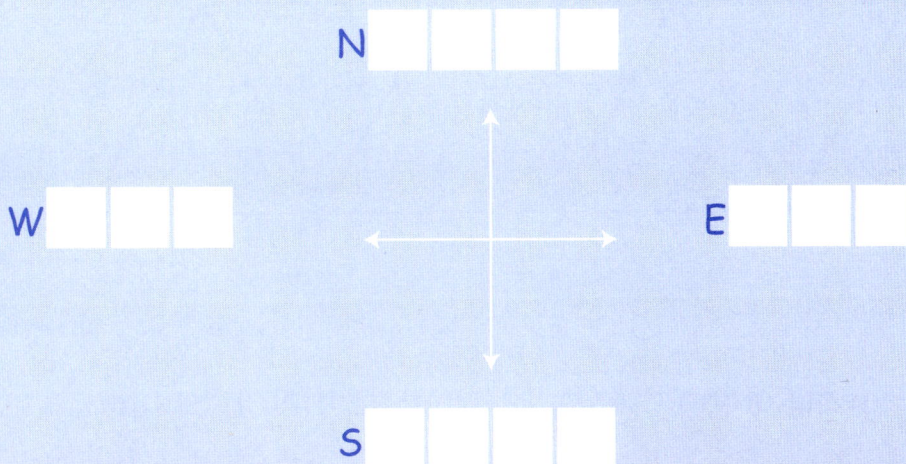

N _____

W _____   E _____

S _____

41

SHAPE INVESTIGATION

TRIANGLE SHAPES

Use this triangle to fold and make other shapes.

• Trace this triangle and all the lines on it.

• Then cut it out and crease along the lines.

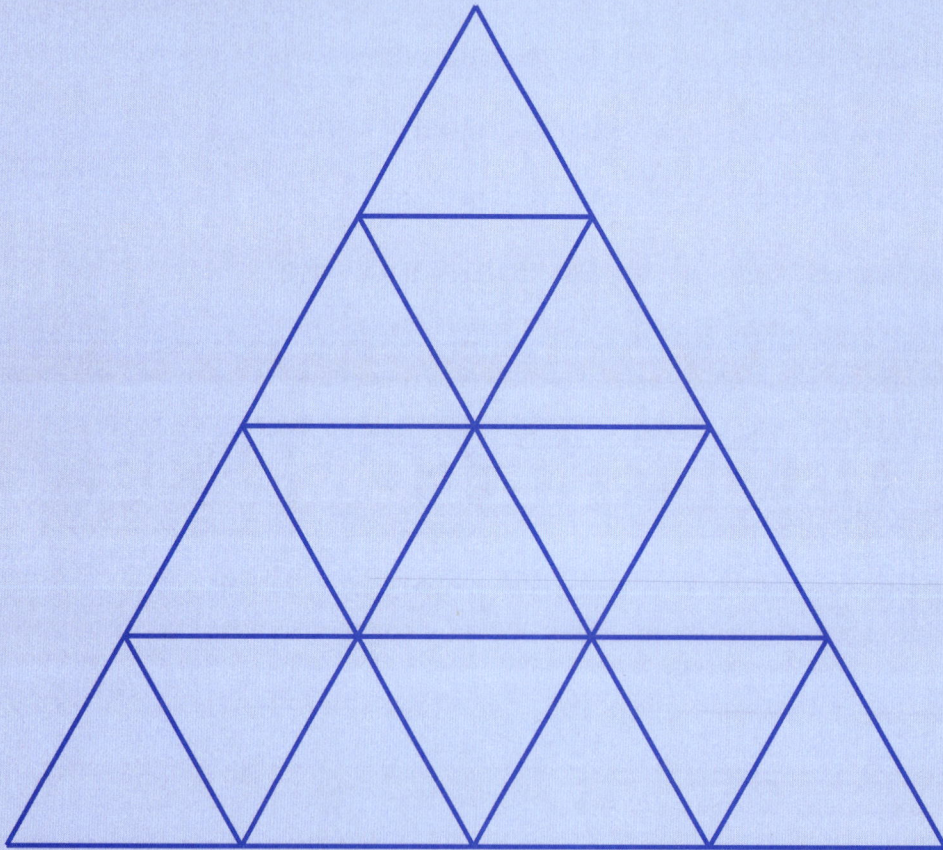

Fold your triangle along the lines to make different shapes.

DIFFERENT SHAPES

Now use your triangle to make these shapes.

1 Two different quadrilaterals

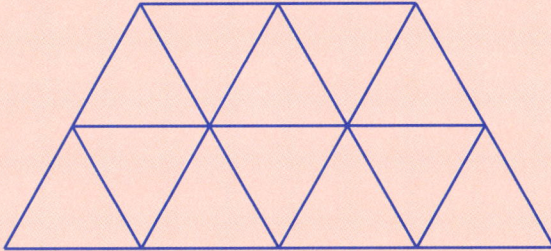

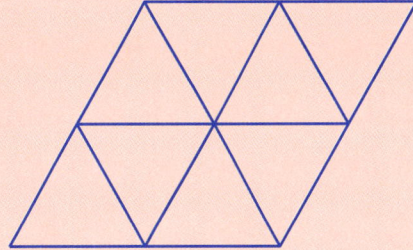

2 Two different hexagons

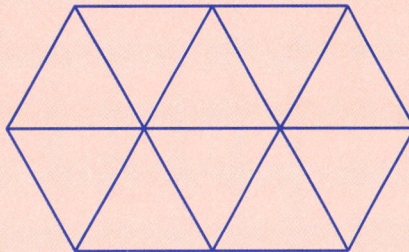

3 A boat

This boat is a heptagon.

A 7-sided boat to sail the 7 seas!

Keep playing with your triangle to see what other shapes you can make.

REVISION TEST

1   Sam has these coins:

(20p) (10p) (5p) (2p)

How much does he have altogether?   [   ] p

2   Draw a line to match each sum to the correct answers.

13 + 5		15
7 + 8		16
15 + 4		18
9 + 7		19

3   Write in the missing number.

14 − [   ] = 8

4   Draw a circle around each odd number.

14   17   25   34   41   50   63

5 This graph shows the favourite fruit of a group of children.

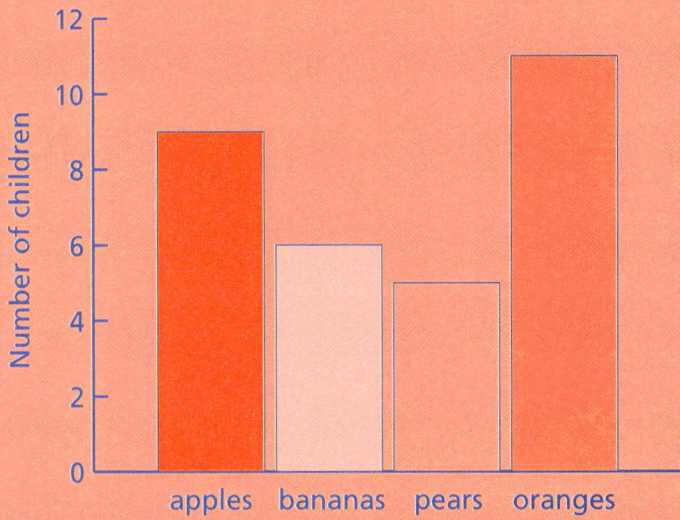

How many children chose pears?

6 How many more children chose oranges than bananas?

7 Colour $\frac{1}{4}$ of this shape.

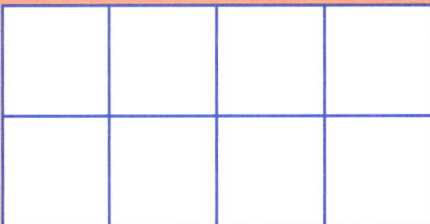

8 Tick the quadrilaterals.

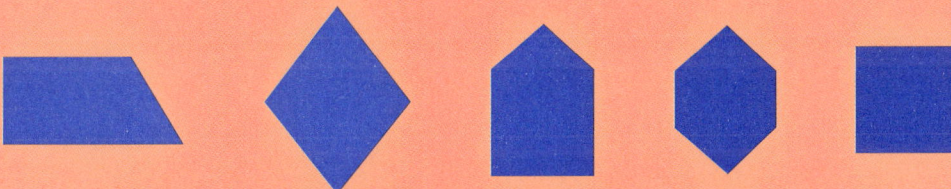

9 Use 2 of these numbers to make 200.

Write the numbers in the boxes.

50   8   100   4   20

[   ] × [   ] = 200

10 2 numbers have a difference of 15.

The larger number is 22.

Write down the other number. [   ]

11 Draw an arrow to show each turn.

start   finish

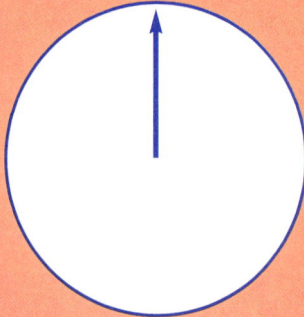

$\frac{1}{4}$ turn anti-clockwise

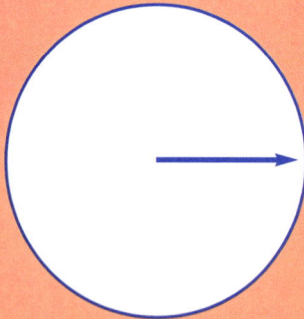

$\frac{1}{4}$ turn clockwise

12 Draw a circle around $\frac{1}{4}$ of these stars.

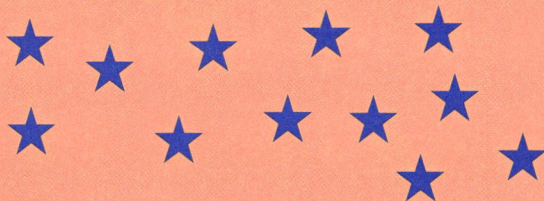

★ ★ ★ ★ ★
★ ★ ★ ★ ★
★ ★

$\frac{1}{4}$ of 12 = ⬜

13 A film started at 7.15pm.

Draw in the hands on this clockface to show the time.

```
      12
   11     1
  10        2
  9          3
   8        4
     7    5
        6
```

`07:15`

14 An ice-lolly costs 15p.

Laura buys 3 ice-lollies.

What change does she get from 50p? ⬜

15 Write these numbers in order, starting with the smallest.

27   45   17   54   61   25

16 Write down 2 of these numbers to make 19.

34 51 46 28 15

☐ – ☐ = 19

17 Draw a line to join these shapes to the correct part of this diagram.

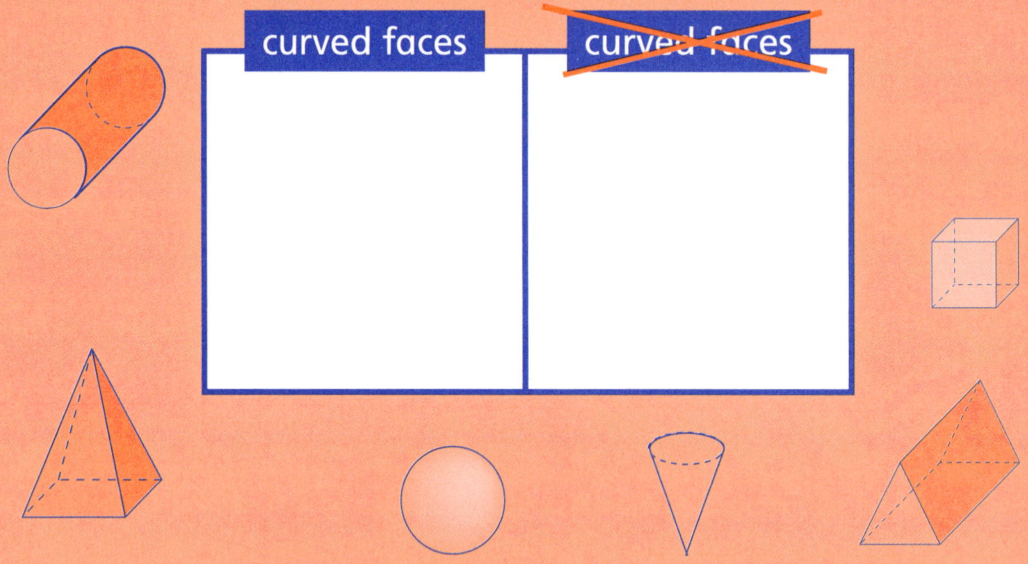

curved faces   ~~curved faces~~

18 Draw a circle around the numbers that can be divided exactly by 5.

18   25   40   32   60   75   52

19 Fill in the boxes to show which numbers went into this machine.

IN DOUBLE OUT

14
22
50

20 Fill in the squares to continue this pattern.

| 9 | 12 | 15 | 18 | | | | |

NUMBERS

Pages 4–5
Counting objects
9 groups of 2 = 18 bugs

Counting to 100

0	1	2	3	4	5	6	7	8	9
10	11	12	13	14	15	16	17	18	19
20	21	22	23	24	25	26	27	28	29
30	31	32	33	34	35	36	37	38	39
40	41	42	43	44	45	46	47	48	49
50	51	52	53	54	55	56	57	58	59
60	61	62	63	64	65	66	67	68	69
70	71	72	73	74	75	76	77	78	79
80	81	82	83	84	85	86	87	88	89
90	91	92	93	94	95	96	97	98	99

Sequences
1 17, 18, 19, 20, 21, 22, 23, 24
2 46, 47, 48, 49, 50, 51, 52, 53
3 32, 31, 30, 29, 28, 27, 26, 25
4 86, 85, 84, 83, 82, 81, 80, 79

Number patterns
1 6, 8, 10, 12, 14, 16, 18, 20 should be circled.
2 30, 35, 40, 45
3 12, 15, 18, 21

Pages 6–7
Teen numbers

```
s i x t e e n
    t w e l v e
f o u r t e e n
      s e v e n t e e n
t h i r t e e n
      n i n e t e e n
```

2-Digit numbers
1 52   2 35   3 64   4 27
5 86   6 43   7 71   8 28

3-Digit numbers
1 487 = 400 + 80 + 7   4 735 = 700 + 30 + 5
2 394 = 300 + 90 + 4   5 918 = 900 + 10 + 8
3 269 = 200 + 60 + 9   6 842 = 800 + 40 + 2

Odd and even numbers
50, 54, 26, 32, 18 should be circled

Multiples

	multiple of 2	not a multiple of 2
multiple of 5	10 20 30 40	5 15 25 35
not a multiple of 5	2 4 6 8 12 14 16 18 22 24 26 28 32 34 36 38	1 3 7 9 11 13 17 19 21 23 27 29 31 33 37 39

They all end in zero.

Pages 8–9
First things first

Comparing numbers
The following numbers should be circled:
1 43   2 81   3 95   4 86
5 64   6 91   7 72   8 87

Halfway numbers
1 21   2 35   3 54   4 20

Ordering numbers
1 19, 24, 25, 27, 30, 31
2 47, 52, 58, 60, 83, 85

Comparing numbers
1 17, 18, 19, 20, 21, 22, 23, 24
2 43, 44, 45, 46, 47, 48, 49, 50
3 80, 79, 78, 77, 76, 75, 74, 73
4 66, 65, 64, 63, 62, 61, 60, 59

Pages 10–11
Good estimates
Buterflies: count → 34
Ladybirds: count → 46
Tomatoes: count → 17
Bananas: count → 38

Number lines
1 4, 7   2 22, 29   3 11, 16   4 43, 47

Rounding
Round to 60   Round to 70   Round to 80

63p   65p   76p
55p   66p   81p
57p   71p   84p

NUMBERS CONTINUED

Pages 12–13
Fractions of shapes

1

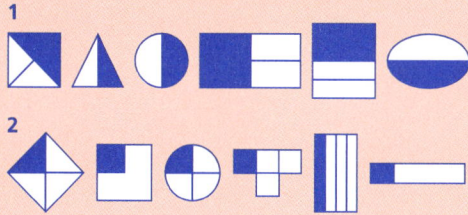

2

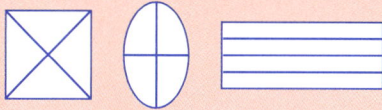

Equal parts
The following shapes should be ticked:

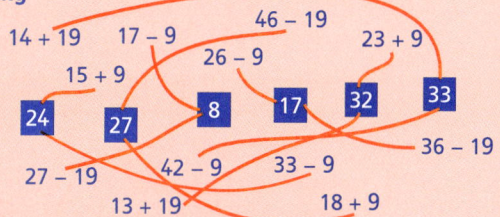

Fractions of amounts

1	3	**2**	5	**3**	4	**4**	6
5	2	**6**	3	**7**	5	**8**	4

Pages 14–15
Complete the square

100	99	98	97	96	95	94	93	92	91
90	89	88	87	86	85	84	83	82	81
80	79	78	77	76	75	74	73	72	71
70	69	68	67	66	65	64	63	62	61
60	59	58	57	56	55	54	53	52	51
50	49	48	47	46	45	44	43	42	41
40	39	38	37	36	35	34	33	32	31
30	29	28	27	26	25	24	23	22	21
20	19	18	17	16	15	14	13	12	11
10	9	8	7	6	5	4	3	2	1

And this one!

1	20	21	40	41	60	61	80	81	100
2	19	22	39	42	59	62	79	82	99
3	18	23	38	43	58	63	78	83	98
4	17	24	37	44	57	64	77	84	97
5	16	25	36	45	56	65	76	85	96
6	15	26	35	46	55	66	75	86	95
7	14	27	34	47	54	67	74	87	94
8	13	28	33	48	53	68	73	88	93
9	12	29	32	49	52	69	72	89	92
10	11	30	31	50	51	70	71	90	91

CALCULATIONS

Pages 16–17
Totals to 10

10 = 3 + 7, 10 + 0, 6 + 4, 5 + 5, 2 + 8
9 = 8 + 1, 4 + 5, 0 + 9, 2 + 7, 3 + 6

Trios

1 4 + 7 = 11   7 + 4 = 11   11 – 7 = 4   11 – 4 = 7
2 8 + 6 = 14   6 + 8 = 14   14 – 8 = 6   14 – 6 = 8
3 9 + 7 = 16   7 + 9 = 16   16 – 9 = 7   16 – 7 = 9

Number bonds

1 14, 11, 16, 16, 10, 17 = CARROT
2 17, 15, 16, 8, 13, 9 = TURNIP
3 9, 10, 17, 11, 17, 10 = POTATO
4 12, 9, 16, 10, 15, 17, 12 = SPROUTS
5 9, 11, 16, 12, 8, 13, 9 = PARSNIP

Pages 18–19
Big numbers

1 50   130   110   160
2 80   30   120   40
3 500   300   1200   1900
4 700   800   300   200

Using doubles

1	28	29	**4**	70	71
2	42	43	**5**	50	49
3	120	119	**6**	80	81

Rounding

14 + 19   17 – 9   46 – 19   23 + 9
15 + 9   26 – 9
24   27   8   17   32   33
36 – 19
27 – 19   42 – 9   33 – 9
13 + 19   18 + 9

Adding 2 digit numbers

1	43	**2**	72	**3**	82
4	74	**5**	61	**6**	88

Counting on

1	9	**2**	14	**3**	17
4	14	**5**	19	**6**	19

51

CALCULATIONS CONTINUED

Pages 20–21
Counting groups
1 $4 \times 3 = 12$ 2 $5 \times 4 = 20$

Dividing
1 6 groups of 2 $12 \div 2 = 6$
2 5 groups of 3 $15 \div 3 = 5$
3 4 groups of 4 $16 \div 4 = 4$
4 4 groups of 3 $12 \div 3 = 4$
5 3 groups of 5 $15 \div 5 = 3$
6 3 groups of 4 $12 \div 4 = 3$

Pages 22–23
2 times table
1 4, 6, 8, 10, 12, 14, 16, 18 and 20 should coloured in.
2 $4 \times 2 = 8$ $7 \times 2 = 14$ $2 \times 3 = 6$
4 $5 \times 2 = 10$ $2 \times 9 = 18$ $8 \times 2 = 16$
$10 \times 2 = 20$ $2 \times 2 = 4$ $2 \times 6 = 12$

Multiplying by 5 and 10

IN	3	9	8	5	7	6	2	4
OUT	15	45	40	25	35	30	10	20

IN	6	7	4	5	9	2	8	3
OUT	60	70	40	50	90	20	80	30

Multiplying by 3 and 4
1 15 → 18 → 21 → 24 → 27 → 30
20 → 24 → 28 → 32 → 36 → 40
2 $3 \times 4 = 12$ $4 \times 8 = 32$ $2 \times 3 = 6$
$5 \times 4 = 20$ $3 \times 7 = 21$ $4 \times 9 = 36$
$9 \times 3 = 27$ $6 \times 4 = 24$ $8 \times 3 = 24$

Tricky tables

1

×	3	2	5
7	21	14	35
4	12	8	20
9	27	18	45

2

×	4	10	3
6	24	60	18
8	32	80	24
5	20	50	15

3

×	8	9	7
5	40	45	35
3	24	27	21
4	32	36	28

Pages 24–25
Word problems
1 90cm   4 9 eggs
2 9 stickers   5 7 sweets
3 4 cars   6 14kg

Money totals
1 £1.72   172p   2 £3.13   313p
3 £2.59   259p   4 £1.95   195p

Giving change
1 35p   2 60p   3 15p
4 85p   5 21p   6 46p

Pages 26–27
What's the postage?
Many answers are possible. Check the child's answers.

How many coins?
1 50p and 2p   2 50p, 10p and 10p
3 50p, 2p and 1p

GRAPHS AND CHARTS

Pages 28–29
Venn diagrams

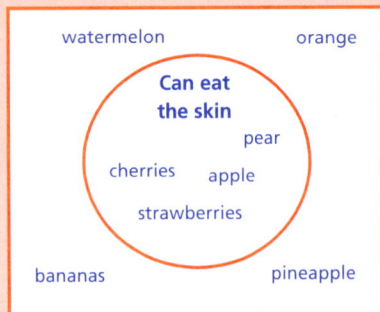

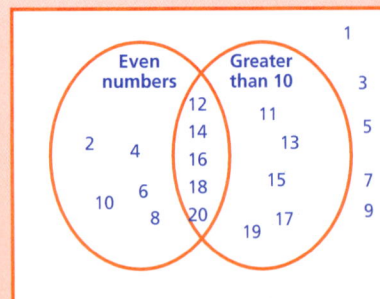

Carroll diagrams

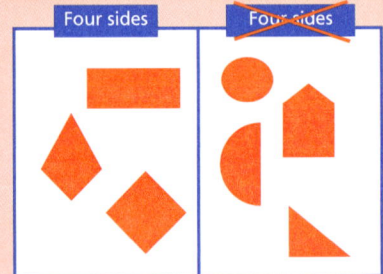

Tree diagrams
1 B   2 C   3 A
4 D   5 D   6 A

Pages 30–31
Pictograms
1 9 books   4 David and Katy
2 Ben   5 12 books
3 7 books   6 3 children

Block graphs
1 5   2 3   3 11   4 28

Bar charts
1 Tuesday   2 9 minutes
3 6 minutes   4 Monday

Pages 32–33
Check children's results.

MEASURES AND SHAPES

Pages 34–35
Units of measurement

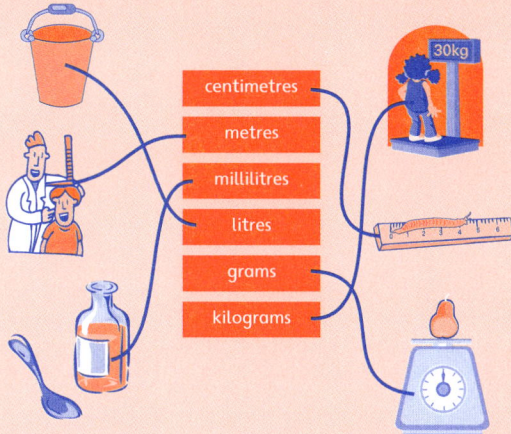

Heavier or lighter?

Longer or shorter?

1	3cm	2	5cm	3	6cm
4	7cm	5	9cm		

Pages 36–37
Time facts

60 minutes = 1 hour	7 days = 1 week
12 months = 1 year	60 seconds = 1 minute
24 hours = 1 day	52 week = 1 year

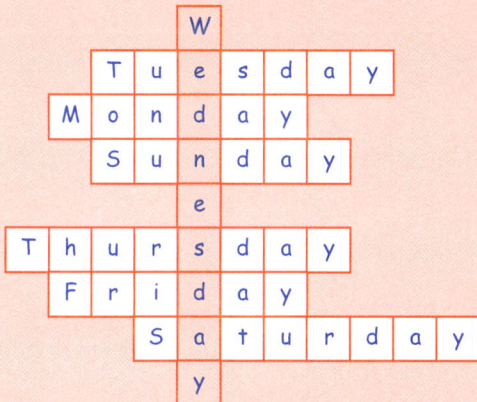

Spring	Summer	Autumn	Winter
March	June	September	December
April	July	October	January
May	August	November	February

Reading the time

1	7.00	2	4.30	3	8.15	4	10.30
5	5.45	6	11.15	7	9.00		

1   2

3   4

Page 38–39
Shape names

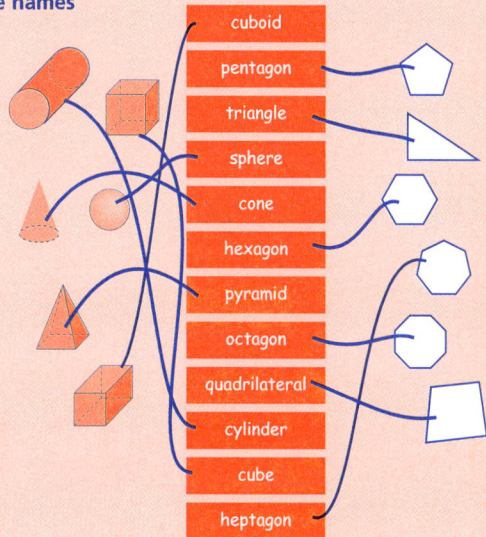

Sorting shapes

1

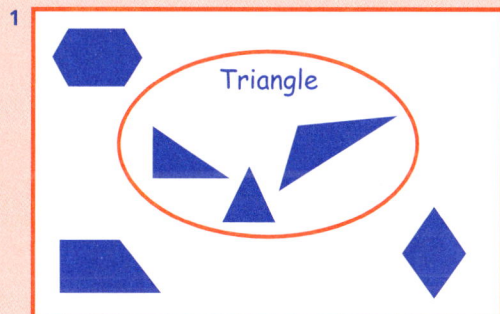

Triangle

2

Pyramid   Pyramid

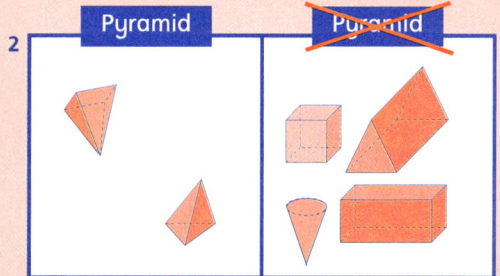

Symmetry

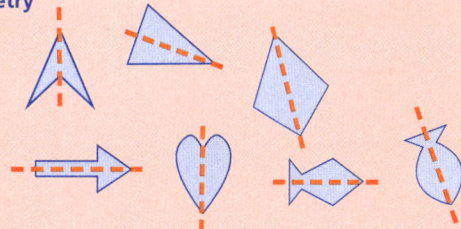

MEASURES AND SHAPES CONTD

Pages 40–41
Grids

1. B6 → car   E2 → horse
    A4 → cat   B3 → tree

2.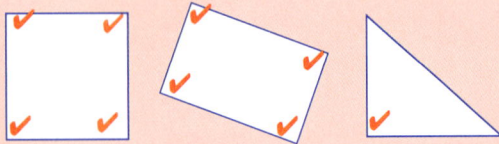

Directions
1 park   2 church
3 church   4 park

Points of the Compass

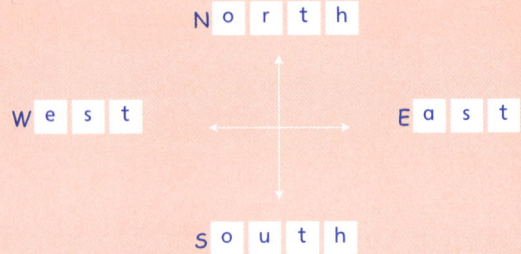

Right angles

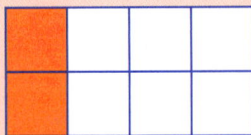

Pages 42–43
Check children's shapes.

REVISION TEST

Pages 44–49 Test Practice

1   37p

2
13 + 5	15
7 + 8	16
15 + 4	18
9 + 7	19

3   6

4   17, 25, 41 and 63 should be circled.

5   5

6   5

7

8

9   4 × 50 = 200

10   7

11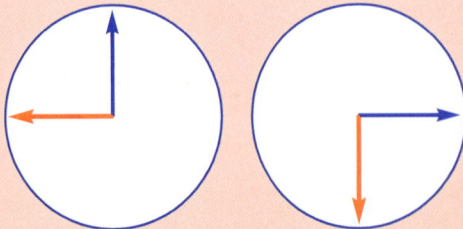

12

$\frac{1}{4}$ of 12 = 3

13

14   5p

15   17   25   27   45   54   61

16   34 – 15 = 19

17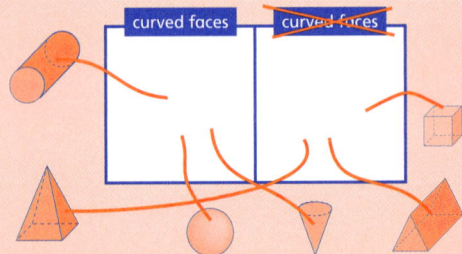

18   25, 40, 60 and 75 should be circled.

19   7, 11 and 25.

20   21, 24, 27, 30.

REALLY USEFUL WORDS

NUMBERS

Approximate A 'rough' answer – near to the real answer.

Digits There are 10 digits: 0 1 2 3 4 5 6 7 8 and 9 that make all the numbers we use.

Dozen Another word for twelve.

Estimate/estimating A good guess.

Even numbers Numbers that can be divided exactly by 2. They end in 0 2 4 6 or 8.

Fraction Part of a whole one.

Half $\frac{1}{2}$ is one half, or one out of two parts.

Multiples A multiple is a number made by multiplying together two other numbers.

Odd numbers Numbers that cannot be divided exactly by 2. Odd numbers always end in 1, 3, 5, 7 or 9.

Rounding Changing a number to the nearest ten. A 'round number' is a number ending in zero: 10, 20, 30, 40, 50, 60, 70, 80, 90 or 100.

Sequence A list of numbers which usually has a pattern. They are often numbers written in order.

Total When you add some numbers, the answer is the total.

Zero 0 or nothing.

CALCULATIONS

Addition Adding one amount to another.

Calculation Adding, taking away, multiplying and dividing are all calculations.

Coins The money we use: 1p, 2p, 5p, 10p, 20p, 50p, £1, £2 are all coins.

Divide Share or group. ÷ is the sign for divide.

Double Make something twice as big, or multiply by 2.

Number bonds These are the addition and subtraction facts under 20.

Subtraction Taking one amount away from another.

Trio A set of three.

GRAPHS AND CHARTS

Axis (Plural is axes) The horizontal and vertical lines on a graph.

Bar charts A type of graph that has bars to show amounts.

Block graphs A type of graph where each block means one amount.

Pictograms Graphs that use symbols or pictures, where each symbol represents a certain number of items.

Venn diagram A diagram that shows groups of things by putting circles around them.

MEASURES AND SHAPES

Anticlockwise Turning in this direction, opposite to the hands of a clock.

Capacity The amount of liquid a container holds.

Clockwise Turning in this direction, like the hands of a clock.

Corners Where the edges or sides of shapes meet.

Edges Where two faces of a solid shape meet.

Faces The flat sides of a solid shape.

Heptagon A shape with 7 straight sides.

Hexagon A shape with 6 straight sides.

Length How long an object is – can be measured in centimetres or metres.

Mass The amount of material that makes up an object.

Octagon A shape with 8 straight sides.

Pentagon A shape with 5 straight sides.

Quadrilateral A shape with 4 straight sides.

Right angles A quarter turn. The corner of a square is a right angle.

Scale These are the labelled marks that show an amount on rulers, jugs and weighing scales.

Square A shape with four equal sides.

Symmetrical When two halves of a shape or pattern are identical.

Triangle A shape with 3 straight sides.